Anatomy of a
Winning Culture

Anatomy of a Winning Culture

A Handbook to Help Directors Build a Pathway to High-Performance, Well-Structured Teams

Tom Atencio

To request a full-sized 8.5" x 11" PDF of all the charts, send an email to: WinningCulture21@gmail.com

13-digit ISBN: 978-1-944662-63-9

Publishing date: May 2021

Library of Congress Control Number: 2021907332

Cover Design by Othman Attaf

Dedication

My overwhelming motivation and inspiration to engage in writing such a book comes from my parents.

My father's smart work ethic and his determination to work daily at achieving immediate and future goals was instrumental in my approach to sport and daily life.

To my mother for her persistence and detailed approach to the completion of task. And for her joy of life!

Thank you!

Table of Contents

HALF-TIME

2nd HALF

Introduction

The ingredients to be a successful sports leader begin with always being a good person while always keeping the well-being of the athlete in mind. All decisions are based on a 'Player Based Philosophy,' or in other words, all decisions regarding club policy and procedure are based on what is the most beneficial to the individual player now, and in the future. This usually begins with the leader's own experiences as an athlete.

Leadership begins with self-analysis and accountability before consideration to include other individuals or teams. The leader acknowledges his or her strengths and weaknesses. The analysis is critical but not negative. Setbacks are seen as ways to learn and move on.

Leaders must continually ask themselves, *what is the outcome of each decision and its effect on the athlete*? Therefore, the question of the day becomes: How did I do as a leader? One can only control his or her own actions.

Live in the present, learn from the past, and plan for the future.

Set realistic goals that stretch you as an individual but remain attainable. This allows a progressive pathway to confidence.

With all success comes risk and vulnerability. Try to succeed as opposed to avoid failing. Competitors accept calculated risk and see change as an opportunity. It is OKAY to compete!

Have a plan or pathway: One's individual personality and abilities will determine the complexity or the simplicity.

What it Takes to be a Successful Coach

There are so many hats a coach wears when fully committing to teaching a team. The success of the commitment is determined by team results, team improvement, individual player improvement, retention of players, and the education of parents. The amount of work it takes to be a successful coach/player is at times an unknown. The discovery and enjoyment of the process is day to day.

Before the tryout:

- Recruiting the prospective players/families
  - ◊ Use club resources
  - ◊ Integrity
  - ◊ No false promises
  - ◊ Ask for help
- Invite players/families out to team training (if a player is switching clubs or currently with a club, you must have permission from the Director of Coaching of the player's current club before the player may train with a club)
  - ◊ If coaching a new team, begin attending training sessions 1 month before tryouts
- Retaining the current players
- Providing options for players that will not return to the team

Tryout Day 1 and 2:

- Create expectations from the start
- Make tryouts competitive and challenging
- Retain desired players and invite new players into team
- Explore alternative options for players not invited to your team: B' team, older team, another club
- Phone contact and/or email may be used to communicate with all players U14 and older. For players U13 and younger, contact must be made with the parent first not the player

Before Team Meeting:

◊ Choose a manager that will complement your efforts. Be patient through this process.

◊ Be prepared with a yearlong calendar, expectations, club/team rules, travel

Team Meeting:

◊ Within one week after tryout (club)

◊ Be clear with your coaching philosophy. Make sure it complements the club's philosophy.

- Clear expectations regarding training, games, travel, and parent involvement

◊ Use club resources

- If you have not chosen a manager, invite an office member to help with the administration of your team

Before Training Rituals:

- All players dressed in club gear
- Coach dressed in club gear
  ◊ Early arrival to field; team effort when a player is late
  ◊ Players begin training on their own 5v2
  ◊ Task completion to enter training; juggling 100 times
- Communication with parents U14 and under. Communication with players U15 and older

Training:

- Begin with a competitive game; small sided, possession, transition
- Active stretch; this is a good time to set the objective of the practice, ask about the previous league/tournament game
- Speed work
- Continue with session objective; follow topic and include competitive, transition, and to goal
- Field equipment picked up by players specifically
- Give time limits on breaks
- Psychology; use every moment as a moment to influence the team and individuals. Word comments in a way that empowers
- Communication short and sharp
- Communicate with individuals after training
- Make sure all players have a ride home
- Technique, Technique, Technique

Before Game Rituals:

- ◊ All players dressed in club gear
- ◊ Coach dressed in club gear
- ◊ Early arrival to field; team effort when a player is late
- ◊ Players begin training on their own
- ◊ U14 and younger warm-up with training topic. U15 and older, it's optional based on need
- ◊ Captains should be decided based on the benefit to the team; rotate, combo, or set
- ◊ Manager's role defined based on need
- Communication with a parent(s) U14 and younger to clarify Communication directly with player U15 and older
  - ◊ Scouting opposition, calling contacts about opposition
  - ◊ Delivery of pregame information should focus on your team's strengths

Game:

- ◊ Allow players to play
- ◊ Do not coach during the moment; talk to players just after
- ◊ Teach the bench players while play is happening; ask questions
- Halftime talk, use it to make 2-3 points to improve the game; always start with a positive, then critique, then positive.

Post-Game Rituals:

- Warm down
- A few words
- Occasional parent/player meeting to educate parents on the team objectives
- Dismiss and make sure all players have a ride home

Multi Day Tournaments or Showcases:

- Before deciding to attend a tournament, make sure adequate preparation can be established
- Make sure team can properly prepare and set themselves up for success
- FITNESS is a must
- Itineraries out to players/parents a minimum of one week before departure
- Have all players arrive at the hotel by 7:00 p.m. the first night dressed in training gear
- Have a light training session on the day before the first game
- Have breakfast as a team at a specific time
- If there's time, have pregame at the hotel
- Have injured players and players that need to be taped at the field 1.5 hours early to see the trainer
- Change your warmup as the weekend progresses; stretch at hotel, make use of the pool, and light warm-up at the game field
- All players need to spend an hour at the hotel with recovery needs: ice bath, pool, stretching, and plenty of rest

- Players that did not play as much may need to have a more active warm-down than those that played more during the game
- Players that do not start game #3 may need to stretch while not on the field
- Teach teams how to manage the game specifically when tired
- Make use of resources and have games scouted so there are no surprises
- Light warm-down after games
- Injured players see trainers immediately after the game
- Eat a healthy snack within an hour after the game, hydrate throughout the day
- In hot weather, players coming from a cool climate need to have sunscreen on
- Have lunch and dinner brought to the hotel and eat at the hotel
- End each evening with a team meeting going over the most recent game, club rules, team rules, play a game

End of the season party:

- Schedule after each season's conclusion: fall and spring minimum

Evaluations:

- Coach to Player written, reiteration of coaching points made during training and games

Coaching Unknowns:

- When to give your team a break
- When to discipline and applaud the team
- When to have parent meetings
- What system of play
- Where to play players
- Development vs. winning

Coaching Opportunities:

Your motivation will make you a better coach

- Watching games
  - ◊ Watching other coaches
- Accept coaching as profession not a hobby
- Dress professional: no sandals, no different brands
- Invest in your development, licenses, gear
- Do not expect things
- Be accountable
- Recruit for the club within the rules
- Game Day Substitutions

Your motivation will make you a better coach!!

What It Takes to Be a Competitive Player
(Player-Author Influenced)

Team DNA:

Effort, Competitive, Intensity, Professionalism, Dedicated, Play at a High Level, Coaching, Push Each Other

Team Habits:

Professional Appearance at all times; Follow itineraries and schedules; Win the ball and try to go to goal; Nothing 'On' keep possession; Punctuality; Receive the ball with Vision (diagonal vison when in wide positions); Lose the ball, get it back; Defend Together; Read Pressure; Direct Play if on (always look for splits)

Team Style:

Use Width; Play Through Midfield; Take 1 v.1; Shoot (only pass if somebody has a better shot); Effective; Vision; Win Ball as fast as possible. Attack or Possess based on defensive pressure.

Components of the Game:
1. Technique
2. Tactics
3. Psychological
4. Physical
5. Guidance (age 13 and older guidance is essential for functional aspects of the game and career opportunities)

Components Rating/Ranking: (5 Youth National Team (YNT), 4 Identification Programs, 3 Youth National Leagues, 2/1 Average Club

Team Ratings Components: Technique 3-4, Tactics 3, Psychological 3, Physical 3

Team Ranking Components: 1. Psychological, 2. Physical, 3. Technique, 4. Tactics

Team Rules:

1. On time is 5+ minutes early.

2. Training - club training gear is the only gear accepted (this includes sweats); shinguards mandatory. 100 juggles to enter training. Begin warm-up on arrival.

3. Game - arrive in warm-up shirt and club track suit. Bring all club uniform gear.

4. Team meetings - mandatory for players and parents unless otherwise specified. Club gear required.

5. Communication - players communicate with coaches, not parents. Coaches may choose to include parent.

6. Managers will not answer soccer-specific questions. Managers handle off the field details. Any questions referring to the team will be directed to the coach.

7. Footwear - sports slides or running shoes when not wearing cleats.

<u>Details of the Club Soccer Year:</u>

<u>Player Opportunities:</u>

- Player Identification Programs
- Personal training or training on your own outside of club
- Youth National Leagues
- National Camps (USA and others)
- College ID Camps (exposure) and College Soccer
- Travel
- Be accountable for yourself and your team
- Think of soccer not as a hobby but a 'profession' or something serious
- Playing 100% every time you step on the field
- Watching other players to see how you can improve
- Pro in Europe or USA
- Guest Play with older teams (Vertical Integration)
- New players to challenge existing team
- Showcases/Tournaments (generally improves your game)
- Weightlifting and Diet
- Play with talented players

<u>Trials/Tryouts – Day 1 and 2:</u>

- Arrive 10-15 minutes early
- Introduce yourself to the coaches
- Stay focused/confident
- Set high expectations/goals for yourself

- Separate yourself from other players
- Separate yourself from distractions
- Don't be afraid to be the best
- Play with the best players
- Don't lower your playing ability based on other players
- Thank the coaches

Before Team Meeting:
- Prepare questions for the coach
- Prepare questions for teammates
- Make sure you are wearing appropriate club gear
- Arrive 5 minutes early
- Make sure you know where and when meeting is scheduled
- Prepare to be engaged the entire meeting (use restroom, eat proper food, do anything that will allow you to avoid distraction during the meeting)
- Prepare to be in the moment and to only focus on the meeting; if you have something going on outside of the meeting make sure you put it on pause to be fully engaged
- If you had a game before the meeting, be ready to share your thoughts on how the game went
- Put away your phone
- Bring a notebook

Team Meeting:

- Wear club gear
- Arrive early
- Be attentive and fully engaged
- Take notes
- Put away your phone
- Be prepared with questions
- Discuss future plans (tournaments, showcases)
- Discuss previous games
- Discussion Points - team DNA, team strengths and weaknesses
- If held in a hotel, be respectful

Before Training Rituals:

- Get plenty of sleep
- Stay hydrated throughout the day
- Eat well
- Pack club gear and soccer gear, soccer ball, and water bottle
- Be mentally prepared for practice (visualization - think about what you can work on at the practice)
- Listen to your soccer music playlist
- Arrive at practice 15 minutes early
- Greet coach and teammates

- Take care of your body and stretch
- Perform 100 juggles
- Start technical exercise

Training Rituals Team and Individual:

- Come mentally prepared and ready
- Juggles, technical exercise, good active stretching and warm-up
- Interval Training
- Cardiovascular fitness (long-term stamina to short-term power)
- Intense training can be done 1-3 times per week, depending on time of year
- Speed and Agility (with and without the ball)
- Change of Direction, ladder drills, patterns, skill work, cone dribbling exercises, technical work
- Core and Power, Injury Resistance (Balance), bodyweight or Free Weights as resistances
- Hydrate and Stretch
- Work smart throughout the entire training
- Try new things and challenge yourself

Pre-Game Rituals:

- Night Before - carbo load/hydrate, pack bag, set alarms, and know the morning schedule
- Lights out no later than 10:30
- Morning of - eat a good breakfast, go on a walk if it's a later game, make sure you have everything for the game
- Prepare yourself during car ride (music, watch highlights, etc.)
- Arrive to field and greet your team-mates (1 hour early)
- Switch into game mode during warmups
- Listen to what your coach wants you to focus on and think about what has recently been stressed at practices
- Take a deep breath and play

Post-Game Rituals:

- Thank the other team, the referees, and the parents
- Team cool down
- Team talk and cheer
- Round of team high fives to keep everyone feeling positive
- 2 or 3 teammate appreciations
- In the car - recover for the next game (eat a snack and hydrate in the car) and make sure you are ready for the next game
- At home - take a shower, take an ice bath if you have another game the following day, eat healthy (breads, cereals, pasta, fruits, grains, juices, yogurt, milk, and sports drinks), watch your game and see what you can do better next game, take notes.

Multi-Day Tournaments /Showcases:

- Before tournament/showcase - make sure to bring all the necessary equipment, be aware of the itinerary or schedule that you must follow during tournament
- Contact college coaches or other scouts who may be at the games
- Review schedule and research opponents to have better context

During Tournaments:

- Arrive five minutes prior to meetings, lunches, dinners, games.
- Begin your own game ritual before each game
- Put 100% effort into every game and work smart
- Do not overlook games or other teams
- Eat healthy snacks throughout day
- Spend time recovering/resting bodies; this includes ice baths, stretching, rest, etc.
- Make sure to rest during off-time
- Stay involved in team activities
- Communicate with coaches and players
- Get lots of sleep

- Follow itinerary
- Wear club gear
- Respect the hotel
- Eat meals as a team
- Have gear prepared the night before a game
- Longer warm-up before game 1, light warm-ups before games 2+
- Spend some time bonding with each other at the hotel
- Stay hydrated throughout the day
- Stay focused on the tournament/showcase

End Of Season Party:

- Free dress
- Talk about the team's achievements
- Bring trophies
- Individual accomplishments and awards
- Make sure to thank the coach and team manager
- Have good food
- Highlights from season

Tom Atencio

Player Unknowns:

- When to take a break
- What to improve on and how to improve
- When to ask for help from coaches and others
- Accurate self-assessment
- What is your role on the field?
- What is your role off the field?
- How to take advantage of opportunities and situations
- How to utilize breaks and non-club events/opportunities

1st HALF

Segway to Excellence

Understand what we want to see on the field

The importance of creating a successful training environment and willingness to teach

Parent Education and Commitment

Understanding *What it takes*

Recognize Opportunity

Enjoying and understanding the process

Vulnerability and willingness to take a chance

Effort-Based Corrections

Attention to Details Rituals

Players taking themselves seriously

Players Responsible for Their Own Game

By-Products: National Semis, Regional Champion, State Cup Finals, Players in National Team Pools

Creating a Club Wide Plan

Director of Coaching Roles by Month

<u>July/August</u>

Execute curriculum and methodology in trainings and games

- Make sure all teams are prepared for the new soccer year:
  - ◊ Manager
  - ◊ Tournaments in August from the approved tournament list
  - ◊ Evaluate coaches, run sessions, 4X+ per week
  - ◊ Evaluate coaches and players, 2X+ per weekend during games

September/October/November

Tournaments: make sure teams have timely registration and travel from the approved tournament list

- Evaluate coaches, run sessions, 4X+ per week
- Evaluate coaches and players, 2X+ per weekend
- Make sure all teams are prepared for state cup
- Add in speed agility coach

December

- Check in with coaches to see if they have planned sessions in December or Indoor training or tournaments.
- Design and assign coaches to run internal futsal league and/or speed agility or training sessions.
- Make sure teams U11-U14 are prepared for January sessions, including schedule, coach's education on winter topics. Reinforce the club policy and procedures, curriculum, and other needs.

December/January

- Oversee coaches on recruiting, retention of player, and any team issues going into tryouts, specifically coaching changes. Coaching changes require introduction of the new coach at least one month before tryouts (How? – define).

- Remind veteran new coaches to interview possible managers before tryouts.
- Attend, organize, and run tryouts. DOCs reserve the right to pick the last 2 players on every team.
- Organize team meetings within one week after tryouts and have the Year-Long Calendar prepared for these meeting. ALL DOCS in attendance and prepared to talk about their individual program.
- Organize a 'new player meeting' for all new players to the club within one week after tryouts. The New Players would attend the NPM and the TM DOC to attend the NPM. DOC to attend TM if the team's Head Coach needs help.

March

- Prepare for Club Meeting
- Teams are prepared with the new Year-Long Calendar

January/February/March/April/May

Execute curriculum and methodology in trainings and games
- Evaluate coaches, run sessions, 5X+ per week
- Evaluate coaches and players, 4X+ per during games
- Make sure all teams are prepared for state cup, showcases, and tournaments. DOC must oversee coach's preparation and make sure teams are prepared to compete.

- Prepare for nationals and Regionals and State Cup. Oversee each team, run sessions, and assist the individual team.

June/July

Define by age-specific needs, club success, and club holidays. This will vary club to club.

Time expectations: hours per week? This is self-determined.

Communicate with coaches regularly:
- In person
- On the field
- Via emails
- Written evaluations

   *Communicate with membership 1X a month (TeamSnap)

   *Work with the Director of Operations on the College Pathway Program; this includes tracking players, meeting with individual teams; use club-approved paperwork.

Extra Time: Does your time commitment match your results?

Vertical Integration

Progression of Success

Purpose: This document is designed to give a one-year perspective of team preparation and the incorporation of the Vertical Integration (VI) of age groups and levels of play. Each criterion has its own detail.

Previous Year to Tryouts: Returning teams – scout needed players. Returning team new coach – review current players and scout to add needed players. New team – scout previous year to try out and run training sessions.

Previous Year to Tryouts 'Identify Staff': Roles of manager, assistant coaches, and parents (specifically those with kids in the program).

Year-Long Calendar: This needs to be prepared before tryouts and available to incoming players/parents.

Master Calendar for Coaches/Managers: This will be the organizational platform that will allow VI semblance.

Include Parents in the Educational Process: Parents educate parents of VI groups on roles and responsibilities.

Educational Consistency Within Team/Club: Demands and boundaries are understood by managers, parents, and players.

Training and Game Rituals are the Same: Arrival-beginning-middle-end-departure.

Consistent Training Habits Instead of System and Function: Players train with good habits out of transition. Players flow in and out of teams. Less emphasis on system and function; not disregarded but implemented strategically depending on the time of year. Combined age group training will have semblance.

Age Group Head Coaches: Older team head coach leads VI combined sessions. Learning opportunities for younger and older players.

VI Combined Sessions: Older players teach warm-up, rituals, and training expectations.

VI Combined Sessions: Weekly schedule 1x 2004/2005, 1x 2005 only, 1x 2005/2006. This is based on the time of the year.

Strategic Meetings with Team/Players: SWOT, goals, social.

Strategic Meetings with Parents: Updates and buy in.

Communication with Third Parties: (All players are rated red, yellow, and green in regard to running gate), PT, and Doctor.

Targets: 50 games (friendlies, tournaments, state cup, league) for Non-HS players/teams, 35 games for HS players/teams. 160 training sessions for Non-HS players/teams and 120 training sessions for HS players/teams. 95% of sessions included 350-400 touches minimum per player and 35-50 soccer-related sprints per player (5-10-15+ yards).

Second Teams: VI if they are competitive with age group - first team, younger team, and older team. Otherwise, VI with second teams only.

Second Team Players: Bring deserving second team players into first team VI when not conflicting.

Oldest Team Syndrome: Train with college players, U23, USL during periods of the year.

Boys VI: 2010-2009-2008, 2008-2007-2006, 2005-2004-2001/2002/2003 Orange.

Girls VI: 2009-2008-2007-2006-2005-2004-2003-2002/2001.

Results:

- Player retention
- Motivated players at tryouts
- Quality-based larger rosters
- Player accountability
- Self-motivation
- Team positive spirit
- Winning mentality
- Parent cohesion
- Team manager cohesion
- Player cohesion playing for the club not just the team
- Maximized effort

Coaches Hiring and Retention Procedure

Hiring Process:

1. Contact Director of Coaching via email and/or phone

2. Submit Resume complete with references

3. Phone interview

4. In-person interview

5. Reference check

6. Run age-appropriate session(s) for DOC (Director of Coaching)

7. Background check

8. Hire or not hire

Retaining your Head Coach position will be based on the following criteria:

1. Development of players and team
2. Attendance at team training, games, and functions
3. Attendance at club and coaches' meetings
4. Retention of players
5. Ability to draw new players into the team
6. Relative results
7. Soccer coaching credentials
8. Soccer playing credentials
9. Ability to teach age specific
10. Team discipline in accordance with club policies
11. Mixture of fun, development, discipline, and results
12. Communication with parents and Head Coach

Reason for not receiving a Head Coach assignment:

1. Loss of a team and/or multiple players
2. Poor player and/or team development
3. Poor team discipline
4. Poor communication with club directors and team parents/players

5. Poor attendance at team, club, and coaches' sessions and functions

6. Lack of motivation to improve the team and club

7. Poor relative results

Exceptions regarding retaining a Head Coach/coaching position:

1. Family issues

2. Health issues

3. Unexpected problems and issues

4. Regional or National soccer opportunity

5. Opportunities and issues discussed with the DOC

Note on Personal Training:

* Coaches may <u>NOT</u> provide personal training to players in the same age group they are coaching.

Extra Time: Do you maximize your staff and resources toward your ultimate goal?

Club Communication Protocol and Parental Expectations

By agreeing to be a coach, player, or parent of a player for the club, members automatically agree to all policy in the club's bylaws, the club handbook, and any other policies posted on the website.

Communication Protocol

A. Parent to Coach:

All soccer issues that are directly related to practices, games, tournaments, team rules, team/player discipline, and anything else that affects the technical, tactical, psychological, or physical mechanics of the team should be referred to the coach, or assistant coach. If a parent has a serious concern that cannot be handled in a short conversation, they can request a phone conversation as coaches are usually busy before and after training. Anything that cannot be resolved in a short conversation should be referred to one of the Directors of Coaching.

B. Parent to Coach:

Any soccer-related question/issue that is not answered by the team coach should be referred to the Director of Coaching. See contact information for means of communication.

C. Parent to Team Manager:

All soccer issues that are **not** directly related to soccer, i.e., fundraising, fees, paperwork, travel, and anything else related to the administrative part of the game, should be referred to the team manager.

D. Parent to Office Manager:

When a question **not** related to soccer cannot be answered by the team manager, a board member may be contacted.

E. Parent to Board of Directors:

Any grievances not resolved by communication avenues listed above can be referred to the BOD who is in charge of hearing all grievances. To resolve problems, the BOD can mediate issues, refer issues to the board, or convene a committee to address/correct the issue.

Parental Expectations

A. Game:

1. Have children at games 1 hour before kickoff.
2. Be positive at games. The club has no tolerance for poor sideline behavior including negative comments made to opposing parents or players, officials, and tournament/league staff.
3. Support coaches' and referees' decisions.
4. Praise all players during the game.
5. Pick up children on time if not attending.

B. Practice:

1. Have children at practice 10 minutes early.
2. Watch practice as often as possible.
3. Ask your children what was taught at practice.
4. Arrive to pick up your children from practice 5 minutes early.

C. Other Expectations:

1. Parents are expected to help with team fundraising, team activities, tournament organization, travel coordination, and club-assigned activities.
2. Good nutrition can make a 70% difference in a player's performance.
3. Watch soccer with your children.

4. Increase your knowledge of the world's game.
5. Be respectful to opposition.
6. Encourage communication with the coach and the manager.
7. Maintain the integrity of the club and abide by the code of conduct.

FAMILIES ARE WELCOME AT CLUB FUNCTIONS!

Director Evaluation Form for Coaches

1	2 Y E S	3 N O	4	Scoring 1= high(excellent) 4=low (needs development)
				Organization
				Layout of field areas in advance
				Organization of players into teams/groups by color
				Ability to quickly organize and walk/jog through exercise
				Overall organizational Skills
				Demonstration
				Willing to demonstrate
				Willing to participate in practice as necessary
				Ability to present clear and accurate feedback pictures in demonstration and corrections
				Overall effectiveness of demonstration0,
				Feedback
				Ability to make timely stoppages during live play
				Ability to provide accurate and relevant feedback to players
				Simplicity and clarity of feedback
				Ability to correct during live play (recognition of coaching moment)
				Amount of information provided
				Overall effectiveness of feedback
				Field Space
				Playing space provided for success
				Playing space realistic to match conditions
				Playing space provided for technical/tactical challenges
				Players Time On Task
				Time spent listening to explanations or watching demo
				Time participating in live competition
				Game Coaching
				Impact of warm up on team
				Impact of instruction on the team
				Impact of instruction on individual players
				Overall effectiveness of game coaching
				Communication
				Impact of team communication; emails, phone calls, meetings
				Communication with director of coaching
				Communication to manager to provide early information to parents and players
				Overall effectiveness of communication
				General
				Overall impact of training on teams play
				Depth of knowledge demonstrated
				Enthusiasm
				Ability to create a playing environment which develops practice themes through small-sided games and into functional team organization
				Ability to relate to players
				OVERALL IMPACT OF COACH

Comments: (Use constructive feedback and include a general tactic reminder for player)

Extra Time: Is it our responsibility as sports educators to educate everybody that we come in contact with? This includes parents.

Tryout Procedure and Evaluation Process

Procedures Day 1

8:15   Coaches set up fields for 4 v. 4; Cone goals (Only) 40x30, prepare training vests

8:45   Coaches at headquarters to meet players and parents.

9:00   Introduction of all staff by DOC

9:10   Fun Technical Warm-Up and Stretch

9:10   Goalkeepers to keeper training. Ask if any players are specifically trying out for GK

9:25   4 v. 4. Three 5-minute games against different opponents

9:45   Water Break

9:47   8 v. 8. Combine two 4 v. 4 fields; play two 7-minute games

10:10   Goalkeepers return to age groups

10:10   8 v. 8. Split the field into 1/3 and play the width. King of the hill style - two 10-minute games

10:30 11 v. 11 (if needed). Full field filled with bubble players starting. All players must play at this time. Make full teams; change teams rather than players unless you have odd numbers

10:55 Warm-down across the field and a stretch. Congratulate all players. Remind players to wear tryout shirts to the next tryout day

11:00 Dismiss

This will be the procedure for all tryout days; supplement the different times with the same procedure

Day 2

Pick out a topic observed from Day 1and follow the format of Day 1

Evaluation

1. Technical - how is the player with the ball?

2. Tactical - how are the player's decisions with and without the ball?

3. Psychological - how is the player's ability to compete and concentrate? Is the player creative? Is the player a leader?

4. Physical - how is the player's speed, mobility, agility, and strength?

- The evaluation will be 0 – 4 with 4 being highest and 0 being lowest

- U-9 - U-12 A' players must have two+ of the above components to make a team
- U-13 - U-18 A' players must have three+ of the above components to make a team
- Look for intangibles and good habits

Staff Coaches Player Evaluation Rotation

U-9 Boys   U-10 Boys   U-11 Boys   U-12 Boys   U13 Boys

U-9 Girls   U-10 Girls   U-11 Girls   U-12 Girls   U13 Girls

- All Coaches are expected to coach/evaluate the duration of tryouts.
- All Head Coaches are expected to run their own tryouts, with evaluators assisting.
- We will meet and evaluate players after each tryout.
- Players invited to play for a club will be communicated to verbally, by phone call, and/or through a post on the club website.
- Confirmations can take place anytime during the tryout process or after.
- The director will have the final say on the last player of every team. This is seldom used.
- Take a picture of all players at check-in for identification purposes.

Extra Time: Is club integrity determined by being a good person?

Parent Tryout Information

Welcome to the Club Tryouts. A player's desire to have a positive tryout is partially made up of natural ability and learned behavior. The coaching staff believes tryouts are an opportunity to educate players and improve the quality of the club. Players will experience a process that will allow them to be competitive and professional while enjoying the game.

Evaluation

1. Technical - How comfortable the player is with the ball.

2. Tactics - What kind of decisions the player makes with the ball and without the ball.

3. Physical - Pure speed, mobility, agility, and strength.

4. Psychological - Concentration, competitiveness, leadership, and attitude.

Formation of Teams

U-15, U-16, U-17, U-18 and U-19 A' Teams - will be made up of the top players 1-17.

U-15, U-16, U-17, U-18 and U-19 B' Teams - will be made up of the top players 18-35.

U-15, U-16, U-17, U-18 and U-19 C' Teams - will be made up of the top players 35-52.

Notification

1. Coaches' notification of Player Selection will begin on Sunday, November 21 and conclude Tuesday, November 30th.

2. Upon selection to a team, players' confirmation will be processed as soon as possible but no later than Tuesday, November 30th.

3. Players that accept the invitation to play before November 30th may be asked to attend the final day of tryouts November 30th to allow for a proper tryout for other players. These players are not being evaluated at this session.

4. A player may be placed on a B' team and later moved to an A' team.

5. *All players will be notified by phone from a coach upon making a team, or not making a team.*

Mandatory Team Meetings

Each individual team manager will contact all players within one week after tryouts for a mandatory team meeting.

The club will be on a Club Wide break from November 30th to December 13th.

Extra Time: How do you maximize your parent support?

Director Technical Report -Coaching Roles

(The following is a sample report)

March/April, 2013

Submitted by:　　　　**Tom Atencio**

Date:　　　　**April 1, 2013**

Purpose:

1. To update board member on club details

2. To provide feedback for upcoming needs

3. To keep DOC/Coaches and board on the same page

Philosophy:

To communicate with the club board of directors on details from the field to the board room in regard to training, coaches, and club opportunities.

Key Activities / Highlights - February and March 2013:

Team

- Trained Team A, Team B, Team C
- Winter/Spring Leagues
- College Showcase
- Team A wins tournament
- Team B doing well in premiere league
- U15-U17 Winter League begins
- DOC and President Meetings to organize vision meeting
- College Recruiting Meetings in person and via email
- Beach Tournament scheduled for June 8-9

Program

- Attended state meetings
- National League follow-up
- Elected board member
- Meeting with Club X about possible merger
- Elected to Executive National Board
- Vision Meetings (2) off the ground

Upcoming Priorities and Activities:

Club

- National League approval
- Finish describing and demonstrating new curriculum to coaches

Notebook

- Functional conclusions for U15-U18 players

Team

- State Cup
- Players now signing and receiving offers from colleges
- Winter League continues

Coaching

- New curriculum is out and will be demonstrated
- Coaches' Retreat June 7th
- Coaches' evaluations
- Coaching Assignments out early

Training Key Goals and Priorities

- Implement New Curriculum
- Sports Psychology for all teams
- Extra training for state cup preparation

Staff / Coaching Updates:

New Coaches:

Resignations / Terminations:

Assignment Changes (include reason for changes):

Team / Player Incident Report:

(student name) ACL/MCL/Meniscus Knee

Recommendations:

1. Parent Support Group - increase numbers and assign individuals to committees
2. Maximize club success by marketing the club
3. Funding semi-pro team
4. Field Development

Thank you:

- To all coaches
- To all board members

Extra Time: Do you track your successes and improvements?

Soccer-Specific Nutrition

WHAT DO NUTRIENTS DO?

Protein

Yes...you do need protein to help build and repair muscles but that's not its only role. Protein is a part of every cell and helps make hormones and regulate fluids, while also building antibodies to fight infection. This makes protein sound like it is the most important nutrient, but it should only make up about 15-20% of an athlete's diet.

Carbohydrates

The energy food for athletes! Carbohydrates provide energy for working muscles. As a matter of fact, the brain also needs carbs to function properly. All carbs break down into a type of sugar known as glucose, which powers the body. Some carbs (simple sugars) break down faster while other carbs (complex carbs) take longer. Complex carbohydrates (grains, fruits, veggies) come packed with other nutrients the body needs such as vitamins, minerals, and fiber, which makes them a healthier choice.

Your body can store carbohydrates in the muscles and liver. This stored form of carbohydrate is called glycogen. Glycogen stores are very important to athletes because they are used to fuel activities like playing soccer. There are special ways to help your body store more glycogen so your energy stores will last longer (see below). Because carbs are so important, an athlete's diet should include at least 50% of his/her calories from this food group.

Fat

All healthy people need fat!!! It helps carry fat soluble vitamins, makes hormones so your body works right, and even helps pad and protect internal organs. It also has lots of calories which can help provide energy for working muscles during moderate exercise. Choosing the right fat is the key. Healthy fats are those that are liquid at room temperature like olive and canola oil. Fat empties out of the stomach slowly, so it can cause stomach pains and cramping if too much is eaten before a training session or game. A healthy diet holds about 25-30% of calories from fat.

Glycogen Stores

Your muscles use up glycogen (stored carbs) during activity. In order to store more carbohydrates, athletes should regularly eat a diet high in carbohydrates. That means choosing fruits, veggies, and grains like pasta, cereal, and rice at every meal. It is also critical to eat or drink something with carbs within 15-30 minutes after an exercise session. This can boost glycogen stores by 300%. You can drink a sports drink or juice, or eat crackers with peanut butter, etc. Some new research says that having a bit of protein with the carbs after a workout can increase glycogen stores as well as help with protein synthesis (muscle building).

Note: When fully glycogen-loaded we typically only have about 90 mins of high intensity exercise / training before fatigue starts to set in, so making sure to consume foods during half time can be very important - especially for those high intensity sprints needed for the end of a game.

Vitamins and Minerals

These nutrients are found packaged in carbs, fat, and protein. They have no calories or energy value, but they do help your body get energy from foods. If you eat a diet that is balanced and includes fruit, vegetables, whole grains, and protein sources you can get all the vitamins and minerals you need. Strict vegetarians who don't eat any animal products at all will need to take a supplement of vitamin B12 as it is only available in animal products. Taking extra supplements won't give you extra energy, so don't waste your money!

Calcium and Iron

Growing kids need calcium for strong bones. The current recommendation is to consume 3 servings of calcium rich foods daily usually in the form of a dairy product. If you don't like milk, there are other foods you can try. First, you could try adding a little chocolate syrup to your milk (if your parents let you); yogurt comes in all kinds of great flavors and is a great source of calcium, as is cheese (pick partly skim or lower fat). Fortified orange juice is another way to get your calcium. You can also get calcium from many green vegetables such a broccoli.

Iron intake can be a problem for some kids, usually girls. The best sources are animal products like meat (dairy products are not good sources of iron!). Iron helps your body carry oxygen, and if you are anemic (low iron levels) you can feel tired, grumpy, and cold. If you don't eat meat, then you need to make sure to get your iron from other foods like fortified cereal, beans, and dark leafy greens. If you suspect that you are anemic, check with your doctor before taking a supplement.

Water and Other Drinks

Most important of all the nutrients is water. Your body is about 60% water. You need it for digestion, absorbing and transporting nutrients, lubricating joints, and most importantly for the athlete- regulating body temperature. When you work out, your body produces extra heat. To cool down, you sweat. The sweat then evaporates off your skin which helps cool you off. Because athletes tend to sweat more, they need to pay close attention to their fluid intake. Dehydration can cause an athlete to feel sluggish and experience muscle cramps or headaches.

How much should an athlete drink? Urban legend tells us to consume 8 cups of water a day. This probably will work for most people, but athletes may need more especially if it's hot. An athlete can lose 2-3 quarts of water when exercising in warm weather! The American College of Sports Medicine has established guidelines for proper hydration (see box). Athletes who are exercising in the heat for several hours should consider drinking some form of sports drink that will replace lost electrolytes (sodium, potassium).

What about Sports Beverages?

Sport beverages usually contain small amounts of simple carbohydrates as well as sodium and potassium. For events that last over 45-60 minutes or longer, sports drinks have been shown to increase endurance. Having a few ounces at half time may benefit some athletes. If you are in a tournament with several games in one day (especially if it is hot!), a sports drink can help with recovery and build up glycogen stores.

By the way, soda is not a good choice for filling glycogen stores or for drinking to replace fluid loss. It is very high in sugar and can have a negative impact on blood sugar if consumed before a game. Soda packs about 120 calories per serving and has nothing to show for it except calories, which is why it is known as an empty calorie food. It has none of the benefits of other healthy drinks like vitamin C in orange juice or the calcium and protein in skim milk.

ACSM Fluid Guidelines

- Drink at least 16 oz of water or other fluid 2 hours before an event
- Top off by drinking 8-16 ounces of water 15 minutes before an event
- Drink 5-10 ounces every 15-20 minutes of exercise. Use a sports drink if exercise is longer than 60 minutes
- Drink as much as possible within 15 minutes of the end of event or training
- Continue to drink to replace fluids lost through sweat

What should I eat before a game or practice session?

Early morning games or practice sessions:

Make sure to eat a healthy high-carbohydrate dinner and drink extra water the day before. For breakfast, try a light 200-400-calorie meal such as a piece of fruit and yogurt or a bowl of cereal or energy bar. This should be consumed about 1 – 1.5 hours before the event.

Mid-morning to afternoon events:

Eat a high carbohydrate dinner the night before and make sure to drink extra water as well. If you have 3 to 4 hours before your event, you can eat a regular meal such as a larger breakfast or lunch. Make sure to eat foods that are not high in fat like French fries or other deep-fried foods. High fat foods empty out of the stomach slowly and can take longer than 3 hours to digest causing cramping during exercise. You might need to eat a snack before your event if it has been over 3-4 hours since your last meal. 100-200 calories eaten about 1-1.5 hours before will help give you energy.

Evening events:

Make sure to choose healthy high carb meals for both breakfast and lunch. These should be easily digested before an evening event. There may be time for an early dinner, otherwise a small snack should be consumed.

Example of a Tournament Eating Schedule

Games at 9:00 a.m., 1:00 p.m., and 5:00 p.m.

Eat a light breakfast at 6:45 a.m. Cereal and milk and ½ banana or toast with fruit or yogurt and fruit. Drink a large glass of water.

After 9:00 a.m. game, eat ½ to 1 bagel lightly spread with cream cheese or peanut butter and fruit or yogurt with fruit and crackers. Drink fluids such as water or a sports drink.

After 1:00 p.m. game, have ½ sandwich with lean meat, pretzels, and fruit. Drink fluids like a sports drink to stay hydrated.

Sports bars can be eaten between games as well. Choose one that is high in carbs and lower in fat.

What should I eat at mealtime?

Every meal should include several servings of carbohydrates (remember, these include fruit, veggies, and grains like cereal, breads, pasta, rice, etc.), as well as a protein food and a small amount of fat.

Breakfast Ideas:

Egg Sandwich on an English muffin or bagel

Hot or cold cereal with skim milk and fruit

Fruit smoothie with yogurt and fruit

Waffles with fruit or yogurt

Toast with peanut butter

Bagel with light cream cheese and juice

Notice that each breakfast idea has a little protein, fat, and several carbohydrate servings. Don't skip breakfast before your work out or event. Research show that athletes perform longer when breakfast is eaten; even a small amount (100-200 calories) helped increase endurance!

Lunch Ideas:

Same idea as above: protein foods, several carbohydrates, and a little fat.

Sandwich of lean meat (turkey, beef, fish, etc.) on 2 slices whole wheat bread, lettuce and tomato and condiments, with carrot sticks, fresh fruit, pretzels, and a cookie

Pita bread with hummus, cut up veggies, fruit, and pudding

Bowl of pasta with tomato sauce, parmesan cheese, small salad, popsicle

Peanut butter and jelly sandwich, carrots, low-fat chips or chips cooked in healthy oils, grapes, granola bar

Cottage cheese and fruit, crackers, veggie sticks, cookie

Bagel and cream cheese, applesauce, cucumber slices and cherry tomatoes, cookie

* If you really like sugary cereal, while this is not a good choice for breakfast, put a cup in a baggy and eat it as a treat or dessert after lunch. It's probably better than some other dessert choices as it is most likely fortified with vitamins and minerals.

Dinner Ideas

Once again, the idea is to eat a serving of protein foods along with several servings of veggies and grains or starchy foods and a little fat.

Here's an idea: Divide your plate into thirds. Up to 1/3 should come from your protein source and the other 2/3 should be from vegetable sources like veggies and grains or starches and fruit.

Any type of lean chicken, beef, pork, or fish along with a salad or some type of green veggie along with a serving or two of rice, couscous, potatoes, pasta, etc.

Pasta with marinara sauce, salad, bread, and fresh fruit, and a serving of low-fat ice cream

Bean burrito (with or without cheese), corn and zucchini squash, and strawberries

Cheese pizza with a green salad with light Italian salad dressing, and fruit

Snack Ideas

Bowl of cereal (not too sugary!)

Granola bar or energy bar

Fruit and yogurt

Crackers and peanut butter

Bagel with small amount of cream cheese

Fruit smoothie made with yogurt

Sports beverage

Hard-boiled eggs and fruit or crackers

What about desserts and sweets?

Life would be miserable without a little candy, cake, ice cream, or chocolate. A healthy diet still has room for treats! Try the 80/20 rule. If you eat healthy 80% of the time, you can have treats for the other 20%. Most likely that means that you will have several servings of fruits, veggies, and whole grains during the day. When you eat this way, you will have more energy and get all of the nutrients your body needs to perform at its best.

How many calories do I need?

Kids, just like adults, vary in their calorie needs. Most likely you will need between 2100 and 4000 calories depending on how active you are. If you feel tired all the time and you are losing weight (and not trying to), you might not be eating enough. Try eating healthy snacks in between meals. Most active people need to eat about every 4 hours.

Note: Serving size (what should be on the plate at each meal) should include "at least a fist size full" of grain-based carbohydrate. If it's a harder training day then go up to two fist size portions of grains (or a slice of toast, etc.).

Extra Time: Is nutrition a lifestyle or a 'Big Event' adjustment?

Soccer-Specific Weight Training for Time

Training Week with NO Team Training (Summer/Winter/Now)

Sunday	Monday	Tuesday	Wednes-day	Thursday	Friday	Saturday
DAY OFF	Cardio Ball Work	Weights for time	Cardio Ball Work	Weights for time	Cardio Ball Work	Weights for time

Weights for Time (Not for pre-puberty players)

- Seek assistance at your gym for specific weight machines that emphasize specific muscles
- All weight-lifting exercises are to be done on weight machines (Nautilus), not free weights, and no squats
- Some machines may cover two areas of emphasis
- Day 1: Chart all maximum effort (max out) on all machines based on two reps' completion of each machine. After taking your max per machine, calculate 60% of your max per machine and begin to work out on each machine for 1 minute. Max out again after 3 weeks.

Exercises will be split into the Shoulders, Legs, Abdominals, Arms, Back, and Chest

1. Shoulders - Deltoid and Trapezius
2. Legs - Gluteus Maximus, Abductors, Adductors, Hamstrings, Quadriceps, Gastrocnemius, Soleus
3. Abdominals - Lower, Upper, Obliques
4. Arms - Biceps, Triceps, Wrist/Fingers Extensors
5. Back - Latissimus Dorsi, Terres Major, Terres Minor
6. Chest - Pectoral Major, Pectoral Minor, Serratus Minor

Workout Procedure

1. Cardio warm-up - 10-minute mile, preferably on a treadmill, 5-minute stretch
2. Work out with 60% max for 1 minute per machine
3. Stretch 5 minutes
4. Total work out time when maxing out: 85 minutes
5. Total work out time normal: 55 minutes

Extra Time: Should cardiovascular athletes who require explosive interval running include middle distance track fitness into their post weekly training at age 15 years and older?

Injured Player Workout While at Training

Motivated players like to be at team training to continue to be included in team functions. This workout provides the physical satisfaction of a top athlete.

<u>Abs</u>	x2
Crunches (legs at 90)	x20
Full V Ups	x20
Bicycle (R&L=1)	x20
Suitcase Crunch	x20
Scoops	x20
Russian Twist	x20
Leg Raise	x20
Toe Touches (Legs In The Air Together)	x20
Toe Touches (Legs Spread Alternate Sides)	x20
Iron Cross (on back, bring opp leg to opp hand) 10 each side	x20
Scorpion (on stomach, bring opp leg to opp hand)	x20

Tom Atencio

Supermans (Arms and Legs Up Together)	x20
Partner leg throws (middle)	1x30
Partner leg throws (side to side)	1x30

Legs Only

<u>Every 5 yards Down and Back</u>

Squat Jump	x3
Deep Squat	x3
Split Jump	x3

<u>20-Yard Space (down and back)</u>

Lunges Forward

Lunges Backward

Spin Squat

Side Squat Right

Side Squat Left

Right Leg Hop (pause for balance)

Left Leg Hop (pause for balance)

Broad Jump (distance)

Arms Only

Y T W	3x10 each
Push Up Pyramid (push up to press)	10 down to 1 back up to 10
Push Up Circuit (push up, hold up, hold down)	x30 sec each

Med Ball Throws x3

Over Head Throws (B, R, L)	x30 each
Side Throws (R, L)	x30 each
Military Press Throws (R, L)	x30 each

High-Quality Club Environment

Purpose: The teams in focus in this report are competitive U11-U19 teams. The purpose of this document is to learn and implement all successful details regarding training, games, and events with players, managers, and parents. To document all training timing and periodization for individual player workouts. To keep players engaged, competitive, and developing during the soccer year. This document unifies a club's development approach with a working relationship between coaches and directors.

Five Parts of Training: (Arrival-Beginning-Middle-End-Departure)

- **Arrival Rituals and Rhythm:** Players arrive to training 5 minutes early and in club gear with shin guards. Acknowledge each player with 'hello,' 'how are you?'

- **Beginning:** Warm-up that incorporates technique with the ball, injury prevention, running technique, soccer-specific movements, and allows players to be social without losing quality. (See below for sample) 15 minutes

- **Middle:** The middle is the main part of the session that begins with an exercise from Sports Session Planner. 10-15 minutes

- **Middle:** Coach's Discovery Period' to work on specific team needs. 30 minutes

- **Middle:** Continued 'Discovery Period' that implements a competitive game that tests the topic for the session. 30 minutes_

- **End:** Review training session and the remainder of the week's schedule and weekend game/events

- **Departure:** Team cheer and departure

    * The normal training rhythm for club teams is 3 sessions during the week and a game or training session on the weekend. Maintain this rhythm during the year except for scheduled holidays and time off

Weekend Game/Events: It is very important to keep this rhythm during the soccer year. If the team does not have a game, schedule a training session or event

Homework: Home training, Technique, or Team project

Parent Meetings: One time per month updating on our progress and staying in touch. Formally introduce new families

Preparation Testing: Ages 14-19 – one-mile run, 30-yard sprint with and without the ball, 60-yard sprint, and 120 shuttle. This is done every 3 months to test fitness but to also formulate Home Workout. This is also done age appropriately: Ages 11-13 – 30-yard testing for running form mainly; 14-18 – all testing to track fitness for injury prevention

    * add vertical and horizontal jump to add correlation of athleticism in direct comparison with sprinting times.

Warm-Up

Warm-up:

1. 50-100 juggles (on arrival), relative amount to the player's age and technical ability

2. Rondo - 2 neutrals, 3 defenders, remaining players on attack. See Sports Session Planner or video for more detail (after juggles), 5-10 min. These games can vary

3. Active Run 18-yard line and back:

   - Straight run
   - Side to side running each direction
   - Bounding
   - Knee hugs

4. Active Stretch 18-yard line and back:

   - Hamstrings out to 18-yard line and back
   - Open gate out to 18-yard line
   - Close gate back from 18-yard line
   - Quads out to 18-yard line
   - Calves back from 18-yard line

     * hold all stretches 5 sec, jog 3 steps, and repeat

5. Jumps and Dribble:

   - Chop jumps with 3-step sprint/pull and chop with the ball

- Scissors jumps with 3-step sprint/double scissor left and right
- Pull back jumps with 3-step sprint/Pull and push
- Tuck jumps with 2 steps sideways and 2-step sprint/tucks alternating left and right
- Chops with drop step (2 players required)

  * Teach players to use their toes (inside, outside, and bottom) when cutting and dribbling
  * Jumps and sprints are from the end line to the 6-yard line
  * Dribbling is from the end line to the 18-yard line and back

6. Passing:

- Inside of foot one touch; ankle locked, toe up, heel down, and point ankle toward the target on contact with the ball
- Bending inside of the foot. Slice through the middle of the ball with inside of the foot; follow through is away from the target. Plant foot even and next to the ball
- Bending outside of the foot. Slice through the middle of the ball without outside of the foot; follow through away from the target. Plant foot behind the ball and to the side
- Skip passes. Contact the ball on the lower half on the sweet spot of the foot (between shoelaces and outside). Plant foot even with the ball but further away. Back spin

- Chips. Same as above except under the ball more on contact to get height and back spin.
- Shots. Shoelaces, toe down, and plant foot next to the ball.

* All passes 5 right and 5 left or by rhythm
* I will add in driven balls
* I am adding throw-ins this week

Once players learn the warm-up, it should take 15 min max. Game should start before practice begins and juggling should be completed before rondo begins.

MONTH BY MONTH EXPECTATIONS

Purpose: The purpose of this document is to give coaches guidelines with club soccer training rhythm and common team topics during a soccer year. The document will also provide a 'month by month' timing of when topics should be addressed.

Monthly Training Rhythm Ages 10-19:

May	June	July	Aug	Sept	Oct	Nov	Dec	Jan	Feb	Mar
TT all	TT all	TT all	TT all	TT all	TT all	TT all	TT 10-14	TT 10-14	TT 10-14	TT all
			FT	FT	FT				FT	FT
	SA	SA	SA	SA	SA			SA	SA	SA
GK	GK	GK	GK	GK	GK	GK		GK	GK	GK
							Wint	Wint	Wint	Wint
SP					SP	SP				
		WT	WT	WT						
							IF 10-14	IF 10-14		
CPP		CPP						CPP		CPP

TT-Team Training, FT-Functional Training,
SA-Speed Agility, GK-Goalkeeper, Wint-Winter Training,
SP-Sports Psychology, WT-Weight Training,
IF-Internal Futsal, CPP-College Placement Program

* *This schedule does not include holiday breaks and individual team breaks. Under the age of 12, 3-month breaks throughout year and 2-month breaks for 13 years and older. These breaks are never longer than 3 weeks at a time and broken up throughout the year. This is based on climate and location of the club, specifically if it is an outdoor sport or indoor sport.*

Team Training 'TT':

- Training by individual team
- U10-U14 May-April, U15-U18 May-November, March-April
- 2/3 sessions per week (depending on the time of the year and important performance dates)
- 1.5-hour session
- Mandatory for all players
- Club staff teaching all sessions

Functional Training (or by position) 'FT':

- Training by position
- One month per position (Defenders, Midfielders, Forwards)
- Monday, August-October #1 U11-U12, #2 U13-U14
- Monday, February-March #1 U15-U18
- 1.5-hour session
- Mandatory for all players assigned by team coach to the individual position
- Fitness optional for U11-U14 players during functional training month
- Club Directors and Coaching and staff coaches teaching all sessions

Speed and Agility Wednesday 'SA':

- Soccer-Specific fitness with the ball and running technique
- June-October, January-March
- Three sessions each Wednesday: #1 U10-U12, #2 U13-U14, #3 U15-U18

- 1.5-hour session
- Mandatory for all players not involved with Functional Monday
- Club staff teaching all sessions

Goalkeeping Training 'GK':

- One GK coach assigned to 4 GKs by age/ gender
- June-November, January-April
- Two sessions per week: #1 Individual, #2 with team during team training
- 1.5-hour session
- Mandatory for all GKs
- Club Goalkeeper coaches teaching all sessions

Winter Training 'Wint':

- Technical Training on turf, Futsal by age group U10-U14, by individual team U15-U18
  - ◊ December 6-13 - March 1st
  - ◊ Three sessions per week: 2 on turf outside, 1 futsal indoor
  - ◊ 1.5-hour sessions
- Mandatory for all players not playing a second sport (U10-U14); second sport players 2X per week
- U14-U18 players not playing high school soccer are organized into a single training session or join the U14 age group
- Club coaching staff teaching all sessions

Sport Psychology 'SP':

- Working two teams per session
- One month per team November-December, April-May
- 3-4 sessions each Monday and Wednesday
- 1-hour sessions
- Mandatory for all players

Weight Training 'WT':

- Gender- and age-specific weight training
- July-September
- 2-3 sessions per week, 1-2 session per week during other months
- 1-hour sessions

Internal Futsal 'IF':

- Futsal 5v.5 with goalkeepers
- December and January
- No walls
- Futsal ball
- 1 game per week
- 1 hour long
- Players arrive 15 minutes before game time
- Mandatory
- Club team coaches and/or Director of Coaching run all games
- Futsal tournament on final game day in January

<u>College Placement Program 'CPP':</u>

- Meet with players and parents 4X per year and individual player meetings by request
- January, March, May, and July
- Meeting #1 – college recruitment process by grade in school. Personal resumes and cover letters
- Meeting #2 – college financial opportunities academically, athletically, and other
- Meeting #3 – progress by each player per grade year
- 1 hour long
- Mandatory

College Placement Program Director runs all meetings with guest speakers and per player follow-up all year

<u>*Use of Outside Resources:</u>

- ◊ Team/Age-Specific Home Workout
- ◊ Technical options for non-training days. This is in addition to Home Workout
- Veo Camera use during training and games. Barrow or strategically plan to use by implementing back-to-back games to make use of Veo 4-hour use

Coaches' Year-Long Communication Protocol *(month by month)*

Team Topics:

Follow up with injured player:

- ◊ Inquire about severity the day of the injury
- ◊ Update weekly on injury progress
- • If player is unable to compete, have them participate as volunteer assistant
- • Core work during team training

Individual parent/player communication:

- • When meeting with player individually, meet in a public place or with an adult third party present
- • Parent individual meetings can be one on one.

Tryout communication:

- • Players are contacted by phone concerning a position on the team between day 1 and day 3 of tryouts
- ◊ Cut players will be notified immediately after day 3 or the last tryout day
- ◊ U10-U12 and new players may require talking to parents and players

Schedule changes:

- Two-week minimum notice for changes to training or game schedules

Team social gatherings – parents and players:

- Team gathering one time every six weeks during summer, fall, and spring
- Team gathering a minimum of one time during winter

Team social gathering – Parents:

- Minimum of one time in the summer
- Minimum of one time in the spring

Post-game comments and post-tournament comments:

- Be positive and motivated
- Inform parents and players about the team's progress
- Explain what the team has been working on
- Remind everybody about the upcoming schedule
- End with positive comments

Pre-season schedules:

- ◊ Pre-season is considered May and June for U10-U19 teams
- Year-Long Calendars are to be determined one month before tryouts to provide information to recruits
  - ◊ YLCs are formally distributed within one week after tryouts

Team itinerary for travel trips or tournaments:

- Itinerary required for every trip and/or tournament
- Must be completed and distributed to team a minimum of one week before event

Winter expectation:

- ◊ Soccer-specific players are to attend a minimum of three training sessions per week
- ◊ Multi-sport athletes are to attend a minimum of two sessions per week
- If a player is unable to attend team winter training, that player may ask his/her coach to substitute another training session
- The club will look to invite new recruits into the club winter training

Spring expectation:

- All club teams will play in the spring in various levels depending on club league membership
- All league scheduling conflicts are to be identified and fixed two weeks prior to the beginning of the league
- Teams with conflicts due to multi-sport athletes will look to bring guest players in from other internal club teams

Pre-season team meetings:

Within one week after tryouts:

1. Manager chosen and briefed on responsibilities by club administrator and coach
2. Club and coach's philosophy presented
3. Club expectations for the year explained
4. Year-Long Calendar finalized
5. Known travel presented
6. Known fees presented by manager

End of the season:

- Complete player evaluations within one week after season ends

- Have team party within two weeks after season ends:

1. Thank players, parents, and managers for the year
2. Talk about positives of the season and progress
3. Inform all families on upcoming tryouts and club events in the off season
4. Have family encourage other players not in the club to tryout

Recruiting communication:

- U10-U14 recruit all year long based on league and state recruiting rules:

1. Follow league recruiting policies

When approaching a parent/player: be polite and be informed

When club U15-19 players are playing on high school teams:

◊ Ask all players via email for their high school schedule

◊ Watch all players a minimum of one time

◊ Email players that you watched a minimum of two days after game

◊ Take note of new players for your club while observing games

◊ Inform all players about upcoming tryouts

• Add Sunday club tactical classroom sessions if necessary (most high school leagues do not allow field club play and high school field play simultaneously)

Coaching change transition:

Coach transition begins a minimum of six weeks before tryouts:

1. New coach introduced to parents and players by exiting coach

2. New coach attends a minimum of four training sessions before tryouts

3. New coach meets with players and parents one month before tryouts

Communication with U14 teams the summer before freshman year:

• At tryouts in May of the previous year, players and parents are updated on the transition from U14 to high school and presented a 15-month calendar

• In March, coach updates team on transition from U14 to high school

Communication with U10/U11 teams:

◊ Expectation at tryouts for new parents
◊ Team meeting with board member present to run through Year-Long Calendar

- Chosen manager versed previous to first team meeting on roll and expectations desired by the coach and the club
- Talk to parents after the last game of the weekend during summer
- Talk to parents two times per month during fall and spring
- Email team one time per week with updates during summer, fall, and spring
- Email team two times per month during winter

Communication with college U14-U18:

- January 15th, March 15th, May 15th, and July 15th – check on player's progress
- August – identify college showcase tournaments each team will attend

Communication with U13-U18 Talent Identification Programs: Notify all players of tryout dates and times one month before tryouts

- Explain process to parents and players
- Explain costs to parents

Director

Director communication:

- Call 24 hours ahead of time if not able to attend a meeting, game, or training session
- Make contact with director after tournaments and games 1 day following the conclusion of the event

Manager

Manager communication:

Consistent communication with your manager is imperative to team success. The coach is responsible for team scheduling details; the manager is in charge of implementing and organizing the desired scheduling.

BY CALENDAR YEAR

<u>MAY</u>

Communication with U10-U19 Teams:

◊ Expectation at tryouts for new parents

◊ Team meeting with board member present to run through Year-Long Calendar

• Converse with chosen manager previous to first tryout day in regard to the roll and expectations desired by the coach and the club

• Talk to parents after the last game of the final weekend during summer to assure tryout attendance

Tryout communication with U10-U19:

• Players are contacted by phone or through post on the website, by tryout number not name, about a position on the team between day 1 and day 3 of tryouts.

• Veteran Club players that will be cut are contacted by phone after day 3. Non-Veteran players being cut will be notified immediately after day 3 by phone or posting on website.

◊ U10-U12 require talking to parents and players

Pre-season schedules for U10-U18:

◊ Club Orientation – Meeting All New Players U10-U19 (separate meetings based on age)

◊ Pre-season is considered May/June for U10-U12, and August for U13-U19

- Year-Long Schedules are to be determined one month before tryouts to provide information to recruits
  - ◊ Year-Long Schedules are formally distributed within one week after tryouts

Pre-season team meetings:

- Within one week after tryouts:
  1. Manager chosen and briefed on responsibilities by club administrator and coach (preferably before tryouts manager is assigned)
  2. Club and coach's philosophy presented
  3. Club expectations for the year explained
  4. Known travel presented
  5. Know fees presented by manager

Communication with college U14-U19:

- January 15th, March 15th, May 15th, and July 15th – check on player's progress
- August – identify college showcase tournaments each team will attend.

JUNE

Pre-Season Continued:

- U13-U19 – determine which tournaments are appropriate for continued growth. Most regional and national championships are played during the summer time
  - ◊ U10-U12 – possible local tournament or leagues based on the level of the team

JULY

Communication with U12-U18 Talent:

- Dates and times

Communication with college U14-U18:

- January 15th, March 15th, May 15th, and July 15th – check on player's progress

AUGUST-OCTOBER

- Talk to parents two times per month during fall and spring
- Email team two times per month with updates during summer, fall, and spring
- Email team one time per month during winter

Communication with U14 teams the summer before freshman year:

- At tryouts in May of the previous year, players and parents are updated on the transition from U14/8th graders to high school and presented a 15-month club calendar

Communication with college U14-U18:

- January 15th, March 15th, May 15th, and July 15th – check on player's progress

Winter/Spring expectation:

◊ All club teams will play in the appropriate league

- All league scheduling conflicts are to be identified and fixed two weeks prior to the beginning of the league
- Teams with conflicts due to multi-sport athletes will look to bring guest players in from other internal club teams

NOVEMBER

Winter expectation U10-U14:

- Soccer-specific players are to attend a minimum of three training sessions per week
- Multi-sport athletes are to attend a minimum of two sessions per week
- If a player is unable to attend team winter training, that player may ask his/her coach to substitute another training session with another internal club team
- The club will look to invite new recruits into the club winter training

Communication with college U14-U19:

- January 15th, March 15th, May 15th, and July 15th – check on player's progress

End of Fall season U10-U19:

- Complete player evaluations within one week after season's end

- Have team party within two weeks after fall season ends
1. Thanks players, parents, and managers for the fall
2. Talk about positives of the season and progress
3. Inform players and parents about upcoming winter training

Communication with college U14-U19:

- In November, meet with all players about the club's college placement program

DECEMBER/JANUARY/FEBRUARY

When U15-19 players are playing on high school teams:
- Ask all players via email for their high school schedule
- Watch all players a minimum of one time
- Email players that you watched a minimum of two days after game
- Recruit new players for the club while observing games
- Inform all players about upcoming tryouts

Winter expectations U10-U14:

◊ -Soccer-specific players are to attend a minimum of three training sessions per week

◊ -Multi-sport athletes are to attend a minimum of two sessions per week

- If a player is unable to attend team winter training, that player may ask his/her coach to substitute another training session

- The club will look to invite new recruits into the club winter training

Communication with college U14-U19:

- January 15th, March 15th, May 15th, and July 15th – check on player's progress

MARCH/APRIL

Coach transition begins a minimum of six weeks before tryouts.

1. New coach introduced to parents and players by exiting coach

2. New coach attends a minimum of four training sessions before tryouts

3. New coach meets with players and parents on week before tryouts

APRIL/MAY

End of the season (U10-U19):

- Complete player evaluations within one week after season's end.

- Have team party within two weeks after season's end

1. Thanks players, parents, and managers for the year

2. Talk about positives of the season and progress

3. Inform players and parents about upcoming tryouts and club events in the off season

Club Wide Vertical Integration VI
'Progression of Success'

Purpose: This document is designed to give a one-year perspective of team preparation and the incorporation of the Vertical Integration (VI) of age groups and levels of play. Each criterion has its own detail.

Previous Year to Tryouts: Returning teams – scout needed players. Returning team new coach – review current players and scout to add needed players. New team – scout previous year to try out and run training sessions.

Previous Year to Tryouts 'Identify Staff': Roles of manager, assistant coaches, and parents (specifically those with kids in the program)

Year-Long Calendar: This needs to be prepared before tryouts and available to incoming players/parents.

Master Calendar for Coaches/Managers: This will be the organizational platform that will allow VI semblance.

Include Parents in the Educational Process: Parents educate parents of VI groups on roles and responsibilities.

Educational Consistency Within Team/Club: Demands and boundaries are understood by managers, parents, and players.

Training and Game Rituals are the Same: Arrival-beginning-middle-end-departure.

Consistent Training Habits Instead of System and Function: Players train with good habits out of transition. Players flow in and out of teams. Less emphasis on system and function; not disregarded but implemented strategically depending on the time of year. Combined age group training will have semblance.

Age Group Head Coaches: Older team head coach leads VI combined sessions. Learning opportunities for younger and older players.

VI Combined Sessions: Older players teach warm-up, rituals, and training expectations.

VI Combined Sessions: Weekly schedule 1x 2004/2005, 1x 2005 only, 1x 2005/2006. This is based on the time of the year.

Strategic Meetings with Team/Players: SWOT, goals, social.

Strategic Meetings with Parents: Updates and buy in.

Communication with Third Parties: Trainer for example. All players are rated red (needs professional assistance), yellow (home program to assist) and green (no issues in regard to running gate). Physical Therapist, Sports Psychologist, and Physicians.

Targets: 50 games (friendlies, tournaments, state cup, league) for Non-HS players/teams, 35 games for HS players/teams. 160 training sessions for Non-HS players/teams and 120 training sessions for HS players/teams. 95% of sessions included 350-400 touches minimum per player and 35-50 soccer-related sprints (5-10-15+ yards) per player per session.

Second Teams: VI if they are competitive with age group - first team, younger team, and older team. Otherwise, VI with second teams only.

Second Team Players: Bring deserving second team players into first team VI when not conflicting.

Oldest Team Syndrome U18/U19: Train with college players, U23, USL during periods of the year.

Boys VI: 2010-2009-2008, 2008-2007-2006, 2005-2004-2001/2002/2003 Orange.

Girls VI: 2009-2008-2007-2006-2005-2004-2003-2002/2001.

High Performance Check List Per AGE:

The game is built around good habits out of transition. All club training must have three ingredients: (1) Transition, (2) Goals, (3) Competition. Our teams must be able to apply training methods to the game situation. The results are players that make good soccer decisions regardless of system.

Club Directors will attend coaches' sessions and use film to evaluate each team's individual training development and club development check list quarterly.

Each club session includes:

1. Technical entry to training/game (arrival)
2. Club Warm-up (15 min)
3. Club-specific possession transition game (10 min) *found in club Sports Session Planner)

U-11

Technical

A. Dribbling (7 moves, but not limited to 7)

◊ Chops, Big toe left foot. Big toe right foot.

◊ Chops, Little toe left foot. Little toe right foot.

◊ Pullbacks, Bottom of toes left foot. Bottom of toes right foot.

◊ Pull and Square, Pull Backward Hop-Square left and right foot.

◊ Pull and Push, Pull Backward Hop-Push left and right foot.

◊ Pull and Tuck, Pull Forward Hop-Tuck left and right foot.

◊ Nutmeg. Pass ball between defender's legs.

Always teach dribbling with a change of pace.

B. Passing

◊ Inside of foot, Left and right foot, various distances.

◊ Outside of foot, Left and right foot, various distances.

◊ Chipping, always with a moving ball.

◊ Passing to open up to receive.

Always teach passing to space first.

C. Receiving

◊ Foot, Inside. Outside, and Sole.

◊ Balls in the air - Foot, Thigh, Chest, and Head.

◊ Turning - Inside, Outside, and Sole of the Foot.

◊ Dummies (fake to touch the ball).

◊ Sweeping the ball and Check shoulders for vision.

◊ Shielding (teach but try to avoid shielding. Teach players to face up and have vision forward).

All must be done with movement.

D. Heading

◊ Basic technique.

◊ All service from the hands.

E. Shooting

◊ Power shot, both feet moving ball.

◊ Slotting - Placing shot at close range.

◊ Crossing and Finishing.

Tactical

A. 1 v. 1

1. Attacking - Players must be able to beat an opponent to the left, right and nutmeg.

2. Defending - Forcing an opponent 1 direction, posture, and toes.

3. Arm Wars - Win balls in tight situations.

4. Tackling and Block tackle.

5. Separate the ball from the opposition (body between the ball and opposition).

B. 2 v. 2 and Greater Numbers and Support angles

1. Defending - Cover and transition behind the ball.

2. Attacking - Basic soccer shape (left support, right support, and splits), support, overlaps, and wall passes.

3. Defending Cover See your man-See the ball- No split

C. Playing out of the black

D. Transition. Transition. Transition.

Physical Fitness

A. Fitness must have mobility and agility. No more than 15 minutes per practice with the ball.

B. Correct running form, jumping form, correct change of direction.

Psychological

A. The best training sessions have a mix of fun, work, and learning. It is OK to compete.

B. Teach rules and function at different positions.

U-12

Technical

A. Dribbling

7 moves) Same as U-11, but all moves must be completed from a passing situation.

B. Passing

Same as U-11 but done at two speeds.

Full speed-Relaxed speed.

C. Receiving

Same as U-11 but done at two speeds.

Full speed-Relaxed speed.

D. Turning

With balls out of the air, and on the ground.

Foot, thigh, chest, head.

E. Shooting

Same as U-11, but slotting shot 12 yards and in from the goal.

Same as U-11, but power shot 12 yards and out from the goal.

F. Heading

Same as U-11 but in game situation.

Tactical

A. 1 v. 1, 2 v. 2, and Group Attacking

Same as U-11, but now add in the combination play (wall passes, double passes, overlaps, diagonal runs), and 3-man combinations.

B. 1 v. 1, 2 v. 2, and Group Defending

Same as U-11, but now add greater numbers.

C. Recognize high- and low-pressure situations.

D. Anticipate and organizing pressurized situations in all parts of the field.

Physical

A. Same as U-11, but at speed and change of directions with the ball.

Psychological

A. Same as U-11, but with confidence encouraged with all technical training.

U-13

Technical

A. Dribbling, Passing, Receiving, Turning, Shooting, and Heading

1. Same as U-12, but with restrictions, and combining two or more technical aspects.

2. More competitive, in the form of restrictions and/or opposition.

3. Crossing and Finishing.

Tactical

A. Attacking and Defending

1. Same as U-12, but players need to recognize 1 v. 1, 2 v. 2, and 4 v. 4 in the bigger game.

2. Introduce functional (by position) games that familiarize players with a desired system of play.

Physical

A. Same as U-12, but add in fitness with the ball by increasing field length, and more transition with the ball.

Psychological

A. Competition must be seen as fun. Players must have an appreciation for technique.

B. Begin to travel to high quality tournaments.

U-14

Technical

A. Same as U-13, but increase pressure by passive and live opposition at speed.

Tactical

A. Same as U-13, but introduce functional training (by position), group defending, and group attacking shape.

B. Function within the system of play.

Physical

A. Same as U-13, but add interval training and plyometrics (short physical explosions with and without the ball).

Psychological

A. Competition must be seen as fun. Players must have an appreciation for technique.

B. Travel to high quality tournaments.

U-15 and U-16

<u>Technical</u>

   A. Same as U-14, but all skills -out of the air, on the ground- are completed with high pressure from opposition.

   B. Bending balls, driven balls, and lofted balls.

<u>Tactical</u>

   A. Same as U-14, but add team defending, and team attacking shape.

   B. Identify players' positional strength and function (2 positions maximum).

   C. Game Management.

<u>Physical</u>

   A. Same as U-14, begin winter weightlifting as a team, increase plyometrics. Increase injury prevention exercises. Soccer-specific intervals with and without the ball.

<u>Psychological</u>

   A. Competition throughout training, confidence with good technique.

   B. Begin College Placement Program.

   C. Travel to high quality tournaments.

U-17 and U-18

Technical

A. Refine and concentrate on all technical weaknesses reviewed by each individual coach.

B. Define specific technical function per player and repeat the action.

Tactical

A. Rehearse the functions of specific positions within the system of play.

B. Define specific technical function per player and repeat the action.

Physical

A. Winter weightlifting as a team, increase plyometrics. Increase injury prevention exercises. Soccer-specific intervals with and without the ball.

Psychological

A. Large group training with emphasis on team attacking and defending objectives.

B. Refine and/or complete College Placement Program.

C. Travel to high quality tournaments.

* All teams will know specific passing routines that relate to Defensive third, Middle third, and Attacking third. Encourage creativity. Most creativity is dependent on good vision and good technique.

* The Age-Specific Objectives are stated in an ideal progression. Some teams may need to vary from their age group specifics based on the age and experience of the players.

Extra Time: What is your club's training rhythm?

HALF-TIME

"At half-time, it is sometimes better to say nothing..."

2ND HALF

Club Travel Policy

Purpose

Travel is an important ingredient when developing players. Success while in a diverse situation improves a player's ability to maximize his/her talents regardless of the surroundings. The standards are designed to improve our teams' chances of success and avoid risk management issues. Violations to the described standards shall be disciplined by either the Coach, the Director of Coaching, or in severe cases, the board of directors.

Head Coaches/Assistant Coaches

Reimbursement

1. Travel - is paid by the individual team members. This includes Flights, Trains, Rental Cars, and Mileage for personal vehicle use.

2. Hotel - is paid by the individual team members.

3. Food Expense - is $30 per day, paid by the individual team members. Receipts must be provided to receive reimbursement.

4. Mileage will be paid at a rate of $.35 per mile.

Procedures

1. A Head Coach shall have an individual room unless there is another coach of the same gender staying at the same hotel; in which case there shall be two coaches per hotel room.
2. A Head Coach with an Assistant Coach shall share a room if the coaches are of the same gender.
3. A Head Coach with an Assistant Coach of a different gender shall have separate rooms.
4. No Head Coach or Assistant Coach shall room with the opposite gender unless married to each other.
5. Coaches shall abide by the Coaches Code of Conduct.
6. Head coaches shall communicate with the team manager or chaperone if he/she will be leaving the hotel in the evening.
7. A Head Coach shall be responsible for developing an itinerary for all travel. The itinerary shall cover all activities from the beginning point to the end point of travel including curfew times for all days of travel, no matter if there are games on the following day or not.

Chaperones/Team Managers

Reimbursement

1. Chaperones, if needed for team travel (i.e. U15 and above) are reimbursed, as stated in the Coaches/Assistants Coaches section under Reimbursement for travel cost and lodging cost. No reimbursement will be provided to chaperones for food. For lodging, a chaperone will be reimbursed for one night of travel for every three-night stay, or at one-third of the room cost. Mileage will be paid at a rate of $.35 per mile.

Procedures

1. Team Travel - The team manager will organize all travel arrangements for the individual team unless a Director of Travel has been appointed by the manager.

2. A minimum of one chaperone shall be provided for every eight players. This applies to players who are not staying in a room with at least one of their parents.

3. Chaperones are to ensure that bed checks are done at the designated curfew time. All players should be in their own rooms at this time. Coordinate these checks with the coach to ensure they are being done each night. A walkthrough outside the room shall also be done approximately 30 minutes after curfew.

Players

Financial Commitment

1. Players are responsible for all fees accrued before, during, and after travel as determined by the Team Manager, or the Director of Travel for the team they are traveling with. If a player is playing for a team (permanent team or guest playing), then they are to be considered part of that team during all associated travel. Included are Coaches Reimbursement, Tournament Fees, Hotel Fees, Transportation Fees, Restaurant Food, and miscellaneous.

Procedures

1. Players are to stay in the same hotel as the Head Coach unless it is pre-approved by the Head Coach well in advance of the travel. An exception can be made by the Head Coach if there are siblings and parents attending a tournament and they are staying in different hotels. All exceptions must be approved by the Head Coach. It is expected that there will not be exceptions for U16 and older teams.

2. Players without parents traveling (U-11, U-12, U-13 and U-14) will be placed up to three to a room with a chaperone of the same gender as approved by the Team Manager. Maximum total per room is four (three players plus one chaperone of the same gender). Players may stay with their families in the team hotel.

3. Players U-15 and older may be placed four to a room maximum, unless the hotel room can comfortably accommodate a fifth person. A chaperone will be assigned to each room. It is left to the Head Coach's discretion and the Team Manager's discretion working together to determine room assignments. A minimum of one chaperone (not including the coach) must be provided for every 8 players maximum. Players may stay with their families in the team hotel.

4. Travel Dress Code shall be club sweats or shorts, club shirt, and running shoes. This is applicable at all times when traveling by Car, Bus, Train, or Air and will include travel-related activities such as lunch or dinner functions.

5. Any vandalism while traveling will be the financial responsibility of the individual or individuals involved. See Player Code of Conduct.

6. **Under no circumstances** will a male be in a female's room or a female in a male's room unless they are related (brother and sister) and they are in the same room that their parents are staying in. For example, if a U16 female player is staying in a room with three other players then the brother of the U16 player may not enter the room at any time under any circumstance. If a player is staying in a room with a parent or with a chaperone, then a non-related player of the opposite gender may be in the room provided a parent or chaperone is in the room at all times.

7. **Club curfew will be no later than 10:00 p.m. for all U14 and under teams and no later than 11:00 p.m. for all U15 and older teams.** All players must be in their own rooms at curfew. Players may not stay in a room other than their own after curfew. **It is expected that the coach will specify in the itinerary the curfew for each night of travel and that often the itinerary will designate an earlier curfew then the times designated above.** A coach may extend curfew to midnight for U16 and above teams only if the team does not have a game the following day and only after the coach has discussed the situation with the team's chaperones and all parties agree on the revised curfew time. Under no circumstances shall a coach, team manager, or chaperone set a curfew that is later than the times set above.

Travel Specifications

Standards

1. All Teams will consider <u>air travel</u> when the distance exceeds 6 hours or greater driving time. This is dependent on airport access.

2. Teams will meet at <u>airport check-in</u> 2 hours before departure for domestic flights, and 3 hours before departure for international flights.

3. <u>Vehicle/Car Rental, when possible</u>

   A. Vehicles will be rented based on need, and seating safety standards. Guideline is to not exceed 1 driver/chaperone to every 4 players reimbursed as team expense.

4. <u>Hotel</u>

   A. Two double beds (queen preferred) per room.

   B. Roll away beds pre-ordered if necessary.

   C. In-house restaurant.

   D. Swimming pool (to be used at the discretion of the Coach/Director of Coaching as identified in the itinerary).

   E. Continental Breakfast.

5. All teams will have daily team meetings and team dinners in which all family members are invited.

Itinerary: 2-Day Trip

<u>Friday 5/10</u>

8:00P   Dinner at Hotel

9:00P   Meeting in Tom's room

10:00P   Lights Out

<u>Saturday 5/11</u>

8:30A   Breakfast

9:30A   Walk/Stretch

10:30A   Meeting in Tom's room

12:30P   Lunch at Hotel

2:00P   Meet in lobby and depart to field 3

3:30P   Game

* Return home

Regional Sports Complex RSC

(address)

(Hotel address and phone number)
T:

(Coach's name and mobile number)

(Manager's name and mobile number)

Itinerary: Multi-Day Trip

(Itinerary is mandatory for all players)

Thursday, November 22

Travel to location in club gear and wear throughout the weekend with slides or running shoes.

3:00P	Meet at hotel in training gear
4:00P	Training at hotel
5:45P	Meet in lobby/depart for dinner
6:30P	Dinner (catered at hotel)
8:30P	Team Meeting in lobby
10:00P	Lights out! Electronics powered down for the night (i.e. phones, iPads, computers, etc.)

Friday, November 23

7:00A	Rise and Shine
7:15A	Breakfast in room tbd
7:40A	Meet in lobby/depart to game
9:30A	Game Field #15
12:00P	Lunch at hotel
1:00P	Recovery
6:00P	Dinner at hotel
9:00P	Team Meeting
10:00P	Lights out! Electronics powered down for the night (i.e. phones, iPads, computers, etc.)

Saturday, November 24

8:00A	Rise and Shine
8:30A	Breakfast at room tbd
9:30A	Meet in lobby/depart to field
11:20A	Game Field #19
1:00P	Watch Games/Recovery
1:00P	Lunch at field
2:30P	Return to hotel/Rest
6:00P	Team Dinner at hotel
9:00P	Team Meeting
10:00P	Lights out! Electronics powered down for the night (i.e. phones, iPads, computers, etc.)

Sunday, November 25

7:40A	Rise and Shine
8:10A	Breakfast in room tbd
9:10A	Meet in lobby/depart to field
11:00A	Game field #8
1:00P	Players are free to depart for home

Hotel Information:

(HOTEL NAME AND ADDRESS)

Tournament Venue Information:

(Tournament venue and address)

Contact numbers

(Coach's contact name and mobile number)

(Manager's name and mobile number)

* No Swimming unless coach desires for recovery

Itinerary: International Multi-Day Trip

June 28-July 8

June 28 Friday	Depart SFO 7:35P

June 29 Saturday   Arrive Barcelona 7:50PM, Meet tour guide, Check in Hotel Catalonia Park Guell (light meal at hotel on roof top, pool)

June 30 Sunday   Training at University AM, Sports Psychology late AM, Sight Seeing PM (Club event Plaza Catalunya, Ramblas, Gotico, Beach, Mercado, La Fonda dinner Olympic Port)

July 1 Monday   Game AM (Stadium Tour, Guest Speaker, PM Club event in park; dinner)

July 2 Tuesday   6:00AM Departure, Travel to Lyon by bus late AM, Check into hotel, Meet tour guide (Lunch in Lyon), Women's World Cup Semi's directly to Stadium 9:00PM kickoff

July 3 Wednesday   Game (U13 game v. Lyon U14, U15 waiting) at National Training Center, Sports Psychology, early PM, (Shopping, Food, Fun Lyon, WWC Semi's 9:00PM Kickoff

July 4 Thursday   Training National Training Center Sports Psychology, Testing AM, Guest Speaker, Beach/team building

July 5 Friday 6:00AM

> Depart, Game late AM Geneva Switzerland versus Swiss team, Sightseeing PM (City Tour by bus), Lunch at swiss team, Boat excursion, Dinner and late return to Lyon

July 6 Saturday
> Game (U13 Tournament U14, U15 waiting), Sightseeing all PM, Club event ropes, Segway, other

July 7 Sunday
> City Center Lyon, WWC Final 5:00P

July 8 Monday
> Return Home Arrive Home

Extra Time: How do you maximize your team time while traveling?

Team SWOT Analysis & Goal Setting
(Strengths, Weaknesses, Opportunities, Threats)

STRENGHTHS (6)	WEAKNESSES (5)	OPPORTUNITIES (5)	THREATS (5)
Communication	Player commitment	Win big events	
Technique	Disrespect for time		Commitment
Attacking Shape (finishing)	Heading balls out of the air	or Team B Beating Team A	Injuries
Movement	Numbers in the box	HS Soccer/Other Sports	Intimidation (self)
Better Communication	Forcing the ball	Play better teams	
Good People	Splits/gaps	Undefeated Season	
Speed	Extra effort	College Showcases	HS Soccer/Other Sports
Confidence	Start faster	State Cup	
Restarts		Win champions league	
		Team Defending	
		Extra effort	
		New Players	
		Cliques?	
		Finish when?	

5-Year Goals

D1 College/Pro

National Champions

Add players to improve team

Stay Healthy

1-Year Goals

Win Nationals

300 Juggles (entire team)

Add New Players to Improve Team

National Teams

Committed to College/Pro

Today's (Now) Goals

Win Showcase Events

Finishing

Team Defense

Balls in the air

Commitment defending

Individual SWOT Analysis & Goal Setting
(Strengths, Weaknesses, Opportunities, Threats)

Strengths	Weaknesses	Opportunities	Threats
- Reading the field - I feel like I have a pretty good concept of space and where everyone is - Passing- I think I can play good balls over the top and play people in - Shooting- hard shot - Heading the ball because I am tall - Movement off the ball I think is getting better and making	- Not the best at defense - Dribbling and moves could use work - Getting back on defense can use work - Getting the ball back when I lose it	- Going 100% the whole game and coming back on defense - Keep going- tackle multiple times, get the ball back right when I lose it - Getting more technical and being able to use moves effectively - Checking in to the midfield - Communicating more on the field	-Not achieving my goals - Maybe someone taking my starting position - Injury

Immediate Goals/Today:

Goals - 6 Months:

Goals - 1 year:

Goals - 3 years:

Extra Time: How do you track your athlete's progress and goal-setting year to year?

International Technical Report (Sample)

BARCELONA, LYON, GENEVA

<u>SUBMITTED BY:</u>	Tom Atencio - February 13, 2019
<u>EVENT:</u>	Coach's education and site approval for Europe trip – summer, 2019
<u>TRAVEL DATES:</u>	FEBRUARY 1-8, 2019
<u>EVENT MANAGERS:</u>	Barcelona, Lyon, and Geneva – meet event managers.
<u>SITES:</u>	Barcelona, Spain; Lyon, France; Geneva, Switzerland.
<u>PURPOSE:</u>	to inspect training/game sites, hotels, places of interest, and meet local organizers before summer travel.
<u>PHILOSOPHY:</u>	To assure that the players and the staff will be tested mentally, technically, and physically while abroad. To expose players and staff to international competition and preparation necessary to compete worldwide.

<u>Local Guide Recommendations:</u> Barcelona, Lyon, Geneva.

<u>Hotel in Barcelona 6/29-7/2</u> Good neighborhood, specifically for the summer. We would like to have a roof top (pool) snack upon arrival provided by the hotel on 6/29. 6/30 Breakfast and Lunch Hotel, 7/1 Breakfast, 7/2 Breakfast.

Hotel in Lyon 7/2-7/8. Has all the necessary details to have meetings, pool recovery, and near the training grounds and highway. 7/3 Breakfast and dinner hotel, 7/4 Breakfast and Lunch hotel, 7/5 Breakfast hotel, 7/6 Breakfast and Lunch hotel, 7/7 Breakfast and Lunch hotel.

BARCELONA

Game Schedule - Barcelona: 7/1 AM kickoff, 3 games back-to-back. Lunch at club.

Training Schedule - Barcelona: 6/30 at University near hotel AM.

Meeting Room Needs - Barcelona: 6/30 12:30P, 7/2 9:00AM.

Excursions: 6/30 Plaza Catalunya, Ramblas, Gotico, Mercado Central, dinner at La Fonda in Porto Olympico, 7/1 dinner at Park Guell.

Food: 6/29 snack roof top at hotel late PM, 6/30 B and L hotel D, 7/1 B hotel L Espanyol D Park Guell, 7/2 B hotel L in transit D at Park on the way to WC semi.

LYON

Game Schedule Lyon: 7/3 at Regional Training Center early afternoon, 3 games back-to-back, 7/7 at Regional Training Center AM, 3 games back-to-back.

Training Schedule Lyon: 7/4 at Regional Training Center AM, 7/6 at Regional Training Center late AM.

Meeting Room Needs Lyon: 7/3 1:00 PM, 7/4 10:00 AM.

Excursions: 7/2 WC semi, 7/3 City Center - walk around WC semi, 7/4 Old City tour, 7/6 Club Event to be determined, 7/7 WC final.

Food: 7/2 L in transit D at park on the way to stadium, 7/3 B and Lunch hotel Dinner in Lyon, 7/4 B and L hotel D Lyon, 7/5 B hotel L D Geneva, 7/6 B and L hotel D Lyon, 7/7 B and L hotel D Lyon Confluence.

GENEVA

Game Schedule - Geneva: 7/5 at Geneva Training Ground, Early afternoon games back-to-back, Lunch at club.

Excursion: Bus tour Geneva.

Food: L Geneva, D Geneva.

U11 to U14 Club-wide Team Job Assignments

Job Assignment	Team	Status
#1 - Plant Sale coordination and operation in late winter/early spring of 2007—80% to players 20% to Club.	U12 Girls B'	Nothing done, need to fine team coordinator.
#2 – Perform community service coordination for the entire club. Could be any community service project that is relevant (does not have to be retirement home visit) and could include Special Olympics Involvement.	U14 Boys A'	Earl talked to Janice about this seven months ago. Earl will talk to Janice again to coordinate this.
#3 - Club Celebration to be held in May. Organize everything for the event	U14 Girls A'	Nothing done, need to fine team coordinator.
#4 - Club Project Warm-Up coat drive coordination to be held in the fall and book drive coordination in the spring.	U11 Girls B'	Joanne is coordinating this with Debbie.
#5 – Organize Unity week including jog-a-thon volunteers and club wide B-B-Q after the jog-a-thon. Get sponsor to come and see if we can get someone from sponsor to talk. Build this into a big event. Promotions, prizes, etc.	U11 Girls A'	Nothing done, need to fine team coordinator.
#6 - Organize parent appreciation night – this could be combined with an annual business meeting, or maybe just a parents social in September or October.	U13 Girls A'	Cathy and Peter have exchanged a few e-mails about this but have not discussed this in detail. Schedule for January or February. Need to set a budget.
#7 - Team Spirit Night Coordinator – this has been done in the past at a pizza place in town	U11 Boys A'	Bob is coordinating this. Scheduled for Nov. 1st.
#8 - Organize First Aid Seminars (2/3 per year) and maintain/restock first aid kits for all coaches/teams	U13 Girls B'	Susan has completed first aid kits for U11 to U14. Working on the U15 and older teams.
#9 - Organize, purchase and install a storage shed next to field #1 at Complex. The shed will need to be approved by the Complex, the club will pay for it and it will need to be installed. This would ideally be complete by this summer.	U13 Boys A'	Peter has e-mailed Jim at Complex several times about this and they have not finalized a design.
#10 - Development of Risk Management Program for the Club – this has been started	U14 Boys B'	Nothing done, need to fine team coordinator.
#11 - Poinsettia Sale to be held in Oct./Nov./Dec. of 2006 – Organize and coordinate all work to allow fundraising. 80% of profit to individual player accounts and 20% to club.	U12 Boys A'	Nothing done, need to fine team coordinator.
#12 - Organize U10 Flyer distribution to Beaverton School District Schools (four times a year) working with Andrea.	U11 Boys B'	Nothing done, need to fine team coordinator.

Extra Time: As a director, do you have a guaranteed and clear non-negotiable structure for your program?

Club-Approved Tournaments

1. Tournament 1, Southern California (U12-U14 Boys and Girls) - August 5-7

2. Tournament 1, Northern California (U12-U16 Girls) - August 12-14

3. Tournament 1, Northern California (U12-U16 Boys) - August 20-21 Weekend

4. Tournament 2, Northern California (U12-U18 Boys) - August 12-13

5. Tournament 2, Southern California (U12-U18 Boys) - September 2-4

6. Tournament 2, Southern California (U12-U18 Girls) - August 26-27

7. Tournament 3, Northern California (U12-U15 Boys and Girls) - September 23-24

8. Tournament 4, Northern California (U15-U18 Girls, U16-U18 Boys) - Nov 18-19 and April 28-29

9. Tournament 3, Southern California (U15-U18 Boys and Girls) - November 25-27

10. Tournament 5, Northern California (U12-U14 Boys and Girls) - December 17-18

11. Tournament 6, Northern California (U12-U18 Boys and Girls) - March 4-5

12. Tournament 1, Nevada (U12-U18 Girls, U13-U18 Boys) - March 10-12 Boys, March 17-19 Girls

13. Tournament 6, Northern California (U11-U18 Girls, U13-U18 Boys) - June 10-13

14. Tournament 1, Oregon (U11-U14 Boys and Girls) - May Memorial Day Weekend

15. Tournament 2, Oregon (U14-U18 Girls and U14-U18 Boys) - May Memorial Day Weekend

16. Tournament 7, Northern California (U13-U15 Boys) - July 21-23

17. Tournament 7, Northern California (U16-U18 Boys) - July 22-24

18. Tournament 8, Northern California (U15-U18 Girls) - July 21-23

19. Tournament 8, Northern California (U12-U14 Girls) - July 29-30

20. Tournament 4, Southern California (U15-U18 Boys and Girls) - July 29-31

* Exceptions to the Approved Tournaments must be approved by Director of Coaching

* Tournaments and showcases are predetermined if club is a member of a national league.

Extra Time: Are your year-long periodization calendars age and gender specific?

APPENDIX

Pandemic Training Rhythm

"There's a lot of trial and error in greatness"
"Vulnerability and accountability are essential in leadership"
"Rage to master and learn quickly"

Tom Atencio

Purpose: The purpose of this document is to learn and implement all successful details regarding Zoom conferences with players, managers, and parents. To document all training timing and periodization for individual player workouts. To keep players engaged, competitive, and stimulated during unpredictable world pandemic.

Background: Integrated players back from high school soccer and 8th graders. The normal training rhythm for these teams is 3 sessions during the week and a game or training session on the weekend. This rhythm was maintained during quarantine.

Periodization: Periodization was always in 3-week blocks due to unknown of when return to play would happen. This was maintained during pandemic.

Zoom Rituals and Rhythm: To simplify, the same training/game schedule was kept the entire quarantine with exceptions for normal holidays. Players arrived to each Zoom meeting 5 minutes early and attended in club gear.

Five Parts of Training: Arrival-Beginning-Middle-End-Departure

- **Arrival:** Music playing and agenda on the screen. When music was turned off, players knew the meeting was about to begin.

- **Beginning:** Acknowledge each player with 'hello,' 'how are you?' Immediately play Electronic Solitaire for time and keep records. Sometimes play Game Face.

- **Middle:** The middle is the main part of the session similar to normal training 'Discovery Time.'

- **Middle:** Individual Player Focus 1. What they bring to the team as a person; 2. as an athlete; and, 3. what they CAN bring to the team if they dedicate themselves (potential). Player in focus (player name goes here). Each player gives their opinion on the 3 questions. The player in focus can ask questions or make comments at the end.

- **Middle:** Discussion of specific team topics: DNA, SWOT Analysis, ranking the Components Of The Game as a team, Goals Setting (5 year, 2 year, 1 year, 1 month, Today), Projects 'Global Soccer Pyramid,' ' What It Takes To Be a Competitive Club Player,' Periodization, Age

Appropriate Weight Training, Mentoring New Players and Younger Players, Pathway to Identification/National Team/Pro/College, The Process, The Flow, The Struggle, Finite Detail Versus Following, Self-Realization, Challenge and Attainability, Anatomy Of A Champion, Define Fun, Accepting The Culture, Selective Attention, Triggers, Barriers, and Fuel.

- **End:** Review the remainder of the week's schedule and weekend game/events.

- **Departure:** Music resumes and all players say goodbye at one time.

Weekend Game/Events: Creating a competitive environment with teams through trivia, match analysis, technical ability for time. Expert speakers in soccer component topics: Sports Nutrition, Injury Prevention and how to tape an ankle (all players taped an ankle), Sport Psychology - Anatomy of a Champion. Guidance speakers: U19 National Team player discussing youth development, U20 national Team discussing COVID-19 training and qualification for U20 World Cup, Full National Team discussing youth development in Europe and becoming a pro. Youth player discussing his recruitment process. Other Events: 'In Search of Greatness' movie viewed and analyzed, Dinner Party - all players cooked one item.

Homework: Analyzed and tracked 'Link and Loss' from game film. Submitted questions for guest speakers. Filmed some home workouts. Worked with other teammates on projects.

Profiles and highlight films.

Parent Meetings: One time per month updating on our progress and staying in touch. Many parents would join weekend zooms. Also, introducing new families.

Individual Player Meetings: To assist keeping players on task, update goals and opportunities.

Managers Vertical Integration: Veteran mangers mentored the new managers on our training rhythm, travel protocol, administration duties, and team rules.

Preparation Testing for Outdoor Return To Play: Active warm-up CLEATS, Figure 8- 15 seconds as fast as you can (video), 30-Yard Sprint with the ball and without (video), Mile, current time (report), and Juggling current record (report).

Zoom Physical Training: Used club staff.

Results: 96%+ attendance Zoom Conferences and Outdoor POD or Cohort Training Motivated players, socialization of 'player to player 'coach to player,' known fitness base, soccer component specific understanding, consistent training rhythm, technical efficiency has increased in small groups and individually, players have been able to move forward with recruitment process domestic and abroad, weekend filming to assist with highlight film, exposure on video in club uniform and continued goal setting.

Actual Documents used
during COVID-19 Quarantine

Agenda Zoom Meeting, 6/9/2020

1. How are you doing?

2. Solitaire – team record: 47.16 seconds

3. Individual Player Focus - 1. What they bring to the team as a person; 2. as an athlete; and, 3. what they CAN bring to the team if they dedicate themselves (potential) - and ALL (One take away)

4. Topic: Recovery League and Training Schedule

5. Testing:
   ◊ Active warm-up - CLEATS
   ◊ Figure 8-15 seconds as fast as you can (video)
   ◊ 30-Yard Sprint with the ball and without (video)
   ◊ Mile, current time (report)
   ◊ Juggling current record (report)

6. Weekly Schedule:

6/8	Home Workout
6/9 4:30	Zoom Conference (Topic: Recovery League, Year-Long Calendar, Mentoring), Home Workout
6/10 5:00	Zoom Workout
6/11 4:00	Zoom Workout
6/12	Home Workout
6/13	Cross Training
6/14	OFF

7. Sports Movies:
Miracle, Glory Road, Hoosiers, Remember the Titans, Coach Carter, Escape to Victory, Bend It Like Nora, Rudy, The Blindside, Rocky, Goal (The Dream Begins), McFarland USA, Invictus, Rise and Shine, Borg v. McEnroe

About the Author

Tom Atencio is widely acclaimed as an influential leader who brings success, direction, and structure to United States youth soccer programs. With an illustrious coaching record that includes 31 state championships, 12 regional championships, and 2 national championships, Tom has traveled domestically and globally for soccer-specific education and competition.

During Tom's 25-year career in soccer, he has demonstrated a warrior-mindset commitment to education that includes educational courses in Spain, France, Spain, Holland, Germany, China, Japan, South Korea, Morocco, and throughout the United States.

Professionally, Tom has held positions that include Executive Director, Program Regional Head Coach, United States Soccer Federation A' License, and National Camp staff and scout. He has coached 40+ regional level players, 11+ national level players, and has held several executive board positions.

As a tough competitor, Tom amassed the following credits during his playing years:

- 3X All-League Selection Damien High School
- 2X First Team California Interscholastic Federation CIF Damien High School
- 4-year Starter California State University Fullerton
- 2X First Team All-Conference California State University Fullerton
- First Team All Far-West Region California State University Fullerton
- National Collegiate Senior Bowl Selection California State University Fullerton
- American Professional Soccer League California Kickers and Los Angeles Heat

Tom grew up in Claremont California with his father, Marshall, his mother, Carmen, and his sisters, Susan and Monica, and attended Damien High School. After high school, he attended California State University Fullerton and earned a BA in Political Science. He currently lives in San Francisco, California. He is a connoisseur of fine dining, and a dog lover.

Acknowledgements

Brian Baxter: Amplify Sports Psychology

Kory Bell: Physical Therapist Orthopedic and Fracture Specialist

Belinda Zeidler: Sports nutritionist, Portland State University

Niki Brooks: Injured player workout

All the players, parents, coaches, and staff that I have had the honor of meeting and working with.

Book collaborator, Michelle Hill, *Your Legacy Builder* at Winning Proof, and her team of professionals:

Cover design: Othman Attaf

Proofreader: Richard Dellamorte

Publisher: Drew Becker at Realization Press

Thank you to the San Francisco Elite Academy and for my time in Oregon, Idaho, and Southern California.

Connect with the Author

To secure Tom Atencio to <u>speak</u> at your next team, employee, or leadership meeting, conference, retreat, or convention, to be a <u>guest</u> on your podcast, or to <u>request media interviews</u>:

Email: WinningCulture21@gmail.com

To request a full-sized 8.5" x 11" PDF of all the charts, send an email to:
WinningCulture21@gmail.com

If you're a fan of this book, please tell others...

- Write about *Anatomy of a Winning Culture* on your blog and social media channels.

- Suggest this book to your friends, family, neighbors, and coworkers.

- Write a positive review on Amazon.com.

- Purchase additional copies for your business or sports team, or to give away as gifts.

- Feature Tom Atencio on your radio or television broadcast or your podcast.

Sponsor

Jungo-Sports

Youth soccer in the United States has evolved from a participant sport of the 80's, to a highly organized professional, multibillion dollar industry of today. Opportunities for boys and girls now exist on both the college and professional stage. The dream is real, which requires a greater level of expertise and shared knowledge to match the ambitions and opportunities for today's player. Technology is more important than ever to develop meaningful connection supporting players and coaches in this endeavor. Pathways to sharing ideas and proven methods is vital to raising the standards leading to the next evolution of the game in the U.S.

Michael Mollay, Co-Founder Jungo Sports

www.Jungo-Sports.com

Jungo Sports is the leading app for ratings and feedback supporting player development, identification, and advancement to elite programs both nationally and internationally. Player driven, we connect players to coaches, colleges, and elite platforms on the global stage.

Sponsor

AMPlify Sports Psychology

AMPlifySportPsychology.com

**We help highly motivated athletes
perform at their best when it matters most**

We are passionate about helping athletes, and all those people who
support athletes to continually grow, learn, and evolve, making peak
performance more and more consistent. We believe that mental training
with sport psychology techniques can not only help performance and
increase enjoyment in sports, but also, in life.

AMPlify your Game, AMPlify your Life!

Visit our website for the latest summer camp information.

Brian Baxter, MA Sport Psychology
www.BaxterSports.com / www.AMPlifySportPsychology.com
(503) 309-3347

CPSIA information can be obtained
at www.ICGtesting.com
Printed in the USA
JSHW060634110822
29142JS00002B/10